THE QUALITY ICON: RAJESH SINGH

DR DHEERAJ MEHROTRA

The book is dedicated to one and only:

Kunwar Yasharth- who is always among us!

Kunwar Yasharth is one of the sources of inspiration for the birth of

Kunwar's Global School, Lucknow.

Contents

Preface

The Quality Icon: Rajesh Singh *is a resource to recognise the wonderful work done by Mr Rajesh Singh, the Managing Director of Dayal Group of Companies in Lucknow, India. Known for this down to earth nature, a visionary and dynamic leader who leads by example by setting up quality benchmarks for others to emulate. The book leads by example as a ready reckoner towards the life story which marked the humble beginning to a successful launch through hard work and dedication.*

The book is a live example of commitment, strong belief and dedication which resulted in success as one of the fascinating success stories.

Author

CHAPTER ONE

The Passion

A passion gives an individual a reason to keep learning and work toward mastery. It can often give you a reason to live and work on wonders and, therefore, have new experiences so key to happiness. It gives you something in common with other people and fosters social bonds. I reflect on the idea of PASSION, which is not a hobby but a habit for a few people. Rajesh Singh, a crusader, is a highly inspired individual who encapsulates quality in nearly every phase of life. With around 180 days, my tenure with him has been very fruitful as a part of learning. The interface has been of great interest and fellowship. The working environment under the umbrella of the Dayal Group is so dynamic and employee-friendly. We learn every hour, every moment, with challenges across. All the staff who works under him is fascinated by his exemplary skills and fellowship traits. Motivation and positive language, which he practices, dwell a lot of preparedness among the staff with vigour and good times ahead.

The priority learning is a preface. He is ably supported by his wife, Sunita Singh, an extended Mother to all the Kunwars' studying in the school. My surprises double when she is with the kids around the campus. Her narration is one of the press briefings, explores "I look my Kunwar in Every Child" is the most engaging and friendly statement which gathers the love, care and comfort to the KGites in a big way. All the parents look for the support and the leadership of the beautiful couple, Rajesh and Sunita. The positive vibes they carry express a supporting hand to all at all times. Their presence harnesses collaboration, comfort and composite culture and contributes to success.

Rajesh Singh believes in learning as a priority and supports continuous improvement, a man of words with action. Regular investments for the students is a priority for the school and is hence the implementation integrated with technology, which is no longer a far-fetched exercise.

The contributory deliberations in the school is a regular exercise by the couple. Rajesh brings honour and recognition to the masses with a positive framework in action. He is a man of words; he excels with a contribution by his involvement in every project he undertakes. He is a ready reckoner of present-day politics, economy, and academics; he contributes to excellence in every field via teamwork and talking.

As a quality practitioner by choice, he activates and dwells on learning and experiential teaching as a priority. His attribute as a commander to the army of employees relates to excellence in any project he undertakes.

A true visionary and philanthropist who has constantly worked towards the growth of the community, Rajesh Kumar Singh, Chairman of Kunwar's Global School and Managing Director of the Dayal Group of Companies, has announced that his school will charge only the tuition fees and that too with a reduction of 25% for the upcoming session to provide relief to the struggling parents in testing times. He has also confirmed that the transportation service will be free. The school plays an important role in preparing community leaders in the field of science, arts, business, industry, politics and sports. A digital campus with 100% area covered around the campus for learning and browsing is a smart step in itself.

With the mission towards making children capable of becoming responsible and productive members of a global society where knowledge, skills and attitudes are inculcated in children through learning experiences and opportunities created for them in the school as a priority.

Mr Singh's noble gesture has reportedly drawn criticism from the unaided private schools association of Uttar Pradesh as the idea of reducing the tuition fees hasn't gone well with most of its members. The other school owners who want to continue charging regularly have Mr Singh pressured by the association to withdraw his decision. Amidst the ongoing tussle, it is being told that Mr Singh hasn't started his decision but has withdrawn his name from the association's membership. Following the incident, the Uttar Pradesh Government has restricted all state schools from increasing the tuition fees for the 20-21.

For sure, with time, what one desires, one achieves only after the attributes and in action. Rajesh Singh is an exemplary example of the same. He said, "There are certain universal facts and are least likely to change. Like them, it is also a fact that a child is considered a representative of God. He stands for purity, innocence and unbound potential, yet as parents and grown-ups, we often fail to recognise the same in the hustle of earning bread and butter.

If we realise this failure of ours and take correct measures to let the child become fortunate by letting him come under the guidance of a true educator where he is not only a 'roll number' but an individual who is not devoid of intelligence & wisdom like other brilliant students, if we enhance his capability by breaking the traditional barrier of judging him through a report card, the day is not far when he will grow into an individual with a strong vision and mission of life, he will feel free to make a right choice and opt for a profession that is socially and economically relevant. "

One of his creations, the KGS, also known as Kunwar's Global, is such a choice that he assumes as for sure will reveal the true potential of everyone whosoever becomes a part of it, whether they are the faculty members or the competent children of today. He believes that We've stepped in with a purpose to make a difference because we think - "To make a

difference in someone's life you don't have to be brilliant, rich, beautiful or perfect. You just have to care enough and be there".

An eminent professional, compassionate social worker, Mr Rajesh Singh has gained a prominent position in society due to the exemplary work in his career. His rise to prominence in such a short span can be attributed to his strong willpower, calibre, conviction, dedication and leadership quality.

Extended Family Members: The Joyful Kids of Kunwar's Global School, Lucknow

Born on 8th September 1968, Mr Rajesh Kumar Singh hails from Varanasi and has a humble background. Son of Ram Dayal Singh hails from the city of nawabs Lucknow; he nurtures a sense of pride in his roots that depicts the great tradition and glorious history of Lucknow. Mr Rajesh Kumar Singh always had a soft side *whenever called on the social front, and this cause gained further strength when his son Kunwar left for heavenly abode at the tender age of 20. Mr Rajesh gradually rose to become one of the pioneering social activists and educationists of Lucknow. He has established Kunwar Lives and Kunawar's Educational Foundation in Lucknow in the memory of his son Kunwar to spread education among the young generation, belonging to rural areas, and more specifically, to underprivileged classes of the society. He is also the Managing Director of Dayal Group, the producer of famous movies like 'Anwar' and 'Fareb'.*

CHAPTER TWO

THE BELIEF

As his words count:

"Started my business with a minimum amount of Rs.1 Lac, struggled a lot, I was confident about my aim and determination, so finally achieved my goals day by day. Now I have decided to provide a platform to the next generation to make them successful, to provide them all the support to become successful, which support I couldn't get."

Rajesh Singh converted his 100 crore land initially allocated for a 5-star club into an educational institute that aims to provide education to children belonging to rural areas and, more specifically, to underprivileged classes of the society.

Leaving every profitable business behind he lays importance to the needs of his tiny tots at Kunwar's Global School, Lucknow

A dedicated couple, made for each other is the source of inspiration to so many families.

A proud wife and big support: Mrs Sunita Singh

"Family is not an important thing. It's everything."

As we know, If there's one thing the pandemic has shown us, it's how critical our families are. Our relatives may be loud and crazy, small and introspective, totally conventional or completely unorthodox, but our family is ours and makes up a massive part of who we are. With family playing such a significant role in our identities, it's no wonder that great writers, celebrated thinkers and observant luminaries have had such unique insights into what it means to be a family in totality.

CHAPTER THREE

THE CONNECT

The priority by the gentleman, Rajesh Singh, talks about a culture that talks about a focus. "The COVID-19 pandemic has pushed the world into a recession. For developing countries like ours, even the survival will get difficult for the commoner", quoted Mr Rajesh Kumar Singh. He further said, "As responsible citizens, we must come forward and do whatever we can to save humanity. Reducing 25% tuition fee is only one small step towards my contributions, and I hope it will provide some relief to the parents that are struggling with pay-cuts and layoffs."

Every special occasion he initiates a tree plantation drive
Every he and his students plant more than 10,000 plants

Making Greener Earth a priority by quality initiatives at Kunwar's Global School, Lucknow

At this educational institution, Mr Singh ensured that students were not merely a roll number but treated as unique individuals with exclusive skill-sets. Breaking the traditional barrier of judging a child through a report card, he promoted his vision of "intelligence beyond boundaries".

A humble leadership in action with the staff at Kunwar's Global School, Lucknow

As the name suggests, it is dedicated to all the underprivileged who desire to learn. He converted his 100 crore land initially allocated for a 5-star club into an educational institute. Crores of investment in its promotion, 50 crores of the loan in its construction, Mr Rajesh Kumar Singh donated and sacrificed all for this school. He firmly believes that the young generation can be truly sincere, dedicated and keen to adopt new learning practices if directed in the right path. They can enter any challenging arena and achieve success if they receive focused attention, an inspiring atmosphere and a bit of extra care.

A champion by words and believing in working the talk!

Not only education but through his trust in "Kunwar Lives", Mr Rajesh Singh has also taken an active initiative of the environment by planting thousands of trees and plants in the premises of Kunwars Global school. He urges all students and teachers on every special occasion to plant trees. He has initiated many plantation drives from time to time. He now has acres of land planted with trees, organised several Health Camps and free medicine distribution for underprivileged strata of society. His Intent and strong will of Social Service did not go unnoticed as he was recognised by many foundations, one of which has awarded him with the Honorary Doctorate for his work in the field of social service. He feels that the root cause of all social evils is lack of ethical values which should have been instilled in the children when they were young. It is because of this they have an identity crisis and have no clarity of their roles in society and their set of values. Keeping in mind the different needs of an infant, a kid and a grown-up child is sometimes not easy even for their parents to recognize in the hassle of earning bread and butter. He gave a strong vision to the school of "intelligence beyond boundaries" which in deeper sense means that a child is free to opt any profession.

Work for a social cause.

The school has been named after Mr Singh's late son Kunwar Yasharth. Drawing energy from the memory of Kunwar, Mr Singh has been making notable contributions through various social activities. Rajesh Kumar Singh has been honoured with the prestigious Mahatma Gandhi Samman at the House of Commons, London, conferred by the NRI Association of India for all his noble work. He has been awarded the UP Ratan twice, in 2018 and 2019, for his tremendous contribution to society. Uttar Pradesh Chief Minister Yogi Adityanath has facilitated his outstanding contribution to education. Sri Ram Naik Ji, Governor of Uttar Pradesh, has been recognised and awarded for his general education and social responsibility.

Internationally, he has received the World Icon award from the Prime Minister of Thailand.

CHAPTER FOUR

The Priority : Quality Work Culture

Recently, leading educationist and Chairman of Kunwar Global School, Rajesh Kumar Singh, joined NewsX for an exclusive interview. He shared his unique and personal journey into the field of education. "I didn't enter into education because of some wish to do this. I have worked in many industries, hotels, movies etc. After my son died in 2014, I wanted to contribute. I wanted to do something meaningful and impact the future of children, and that's why I entered into this field."

When Pen speaks to be mightier, the work executes as a result.

He believes in the say,

I always want to be part of the solution and not the problem. Being an entrepreneur who turned a town around, I changed my thought of life.

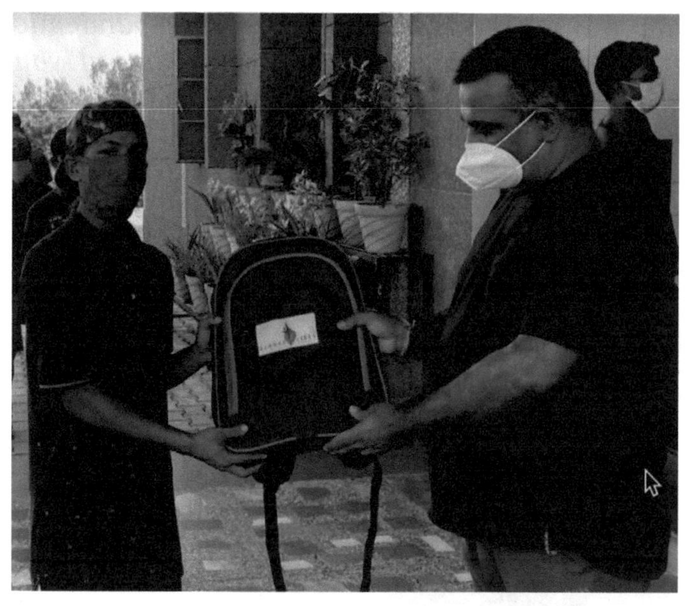

Sharing love and care as a priority

Speaking on the commercialisation of education, Kumar shared his passionately held views on the matter. "The entire educationist and schooling community has acquired a terrible reputation. We're viewed as shopkeepers, just trying to make the most money from people. We need to improve our image and be more like the police forces and the medical professionals.

He views the pandemic as a failed opportunity for the schooling community to have done this and says, "We could have used the pandemic to change public perception, but instead you saw people raising fees, even in the times of coronavirus."

Rajesh Singh adopted several cows in his Dairy farm from the roads He now feeds them and takes good care of them

His school, the Kunwar Global School, has taken a big first step and cut the fees by 25%. "We're the first to do this, to cut the fees by 25% and to move forward with our work."

11,000 Bal Geeta distribution distribution from class 1st to 5th

The government doesn't have a clear policy on education, he feels. He says that the government hasn't decided between private and public education. "Supposedly, schools are built as not-for-profit organisations in our system. Please explain why it is so then that as soon as the school is built, the school managers try to get a franchise? Secondly, if the government wants to allow private education, fine, but then why don't they say 'Ok, you want to run a business, run a business then' and then collect tax from it?"

- Runs a charitable boarding school by the name of Kunwar's Global School also the first school in India to publish its Balance sheet in the annual books everywhere

Speaking on online education during the pandemic, Kumar feels it is necessary. "I don't think it's good, but we don't have a choice. I'm happy that the government has decided to reduce the time of online classes. I still feel, though, that we should give the students homework for a day or two and have at least one class every two days."

- He adopted many school students who were not able to pay the fees due to some or the other reason, handholded them not only for school but until they are self-sufficient and successful in life

He doesn't support the new 'No school, no fees' movement that has been coming up during the pandemic. He says, "I don't support that at all. The school has so many salaries to pay and many costs to bear, gardeners, teachers, etc. Now certainly I think many schools show one amount in their earnings and expenses and earn and spend another, and that is a problem that needs to be solved, but no fees are not an option at all."

He was the first one during Covid Pandemic to initiate biggest fee discount in the school fee charging only the tution fee with only 25% discount

His advice for students is to prioritise their mental health over their studies. He says, "we can catch up with the studies, but we need students to be in the right mindset and frame of mind."

A promoter of NCC and Nation First! Jai Hind

He is extremely sensitive for the students and their health biggest example of which is although being an educationist and running a school in charity he advocated ban on online education till class 5th

Finally, he shares his opinion about the new phase of reopening our economy and country. He feels that "schools need to open' and that currently, many boarding schools have performed their own 'quarantines', where "no one can get in or out". " Reopening the schools will be beneficial, I feel, in the long run."

To save the growing student from adulteration he is maintaining a big organic farm and a dairy farm where he himself takes care of the cows and closely monitors their productivity and purity so that the food given to the students is best edible

CHAPTER FIVE

A QUALITY NOTION

Quote " April 6, 2015- A day, an event, a historical moment for Kunwar's Global School. It was the first day of our school when we had our first assembly. It was as if Kunwar was born again. We could see Kunwars in each child. It started with Sri Ganesh Vandana, followed by prayer and the KGS pledge. The Head Mistress welcomed our children. The chairman congratulated the teachers and children for the beginning of the journey in the KGS Family. He said that education is a never-ending process which needs to be covered with our dedication, passion and hard work."

Unquote.

KGS, popularly known as Kunwar's Global School, strives to provide education founded on excellence and create the broadest range of opportunities for the complete development of students. Kunwar's Global School infuses creative thoughts and ideas in its students. Teaching is imparted beyond the regular classroom curriculum to sow the seeds of students' social commitment, nationalism, and social responsibilities. Welcome to Kunwar's Global School, a school that believes that "Great changes in the destiny of a mankind can be effected only in the minds of little children". In this competitive world, no effort is sufficient; there is always something more to achieve. The desires, ambition, passions are unlimited. We need to hone our potential and deliver it at its best with the time and situation. Abraham Lincoln wonderfully said, "Whatever You are, Be a Good One".

I firmly believe that the success of a school is directly proportional to the happiness quotient of its stakeholders. I prefer Kunwar's Global School to be called a home of happy students and staff rather than being identified only with the success stories of a few individuals. We will all work with unbridled enthusiasm if we collectively create an environment where unnecessary pressure and stress do not impede our progress. We are a team of learners working together to enlighten the young minds wrapped in dreams. Children are a bundle of talents; we help them untie the ribbon. We aim to make our students market-ready, unmasking their capacity of hard work and boundless knowledge to the world. The seeds of discipline that are sown in the hearts and minds of our students help them to germinate into the torch-bearers of tomorrow as people who are

accustomed to success. Kunwar's Global School inhabitants are fortunate to live in an environment conducive to teaching, learning, and overall growth.

While academics are from the core of our curricular structure here, the importance of sports and other activities is never undermined. The school provides new vistas of growth where children can bloom and exploit their potential in myriad ways. As the instructional leader of Kunwar's Global School, I have significant moral, ethical, and legal obligations where all students can achieve their full potential and receive an equal opportunity to succeed in society. I come to Kunwar's Global School with a dream to place it among the top schools globally. This dream can only come true if I teach the Learners attributes of Values, attitudes, motivation, empathy, knowledge and skills in each of my students through a strong team of teachers. I seek the blessings and support of all the stakeholders in accomplishing the vision and the mission of Kunwar's Global School.

The Dayal Group targets quality in any and every initiative it governs. The group conducts all its ambitions with a deep sense of commitment - a commitment to quality, to schedules and most of all to our clients. The

'Dayal Group' needs no introduction in Lucknow & Varanasi in the trade. Business activities started about a decade back because of the persistent, innovative and dynamic efforts of Mr Rajesh Singh, who is the MD of Dayal Group and Chairman of Kunwar's Global School. He was born and brought up in the holy city of Varanasi. He grew up with a healthy, pure, and pious family tradition to work hard and honestly. After post-graduation from Lucknow University, he worked hard to get to this stage. Still, he never lost hope and embarked on a new venture, a project to provide shelter to the needy at much cheaper rates than what development authorities are giving to people in the holy city of Varanasi. His second venture of shops and flats in Varanasi was a great success. The company is working with the trade name - Dayal Group. Rajesh Singh is the Managing Director, who organised the entire things professionally with his past experiences that the group today stands poised as the leading and most recognised business group in India. A person who needs no introduction, Mr Rajesh Singh has constantly been working hard towards the sustainable development of society by creating new opportunities, employment for youth and constant welfare. A renowned social activist, his commitment to the community has helped thousands of poor and backward families live better lives.

A true visionary with a vision to provide free access to Education for all, Mr Rajesh Singh provides Free Education to 25 per cent of the total strength at Kunwar's Global School to students belonging to backward and underprivileged strata of society. Beginning with a small house colony project in Varanasi in the late 90s and now, after six years, the group is considered a promoter of the best housing colony and commercial premises in both the cities. The group has completed residential colonies, commercial premises and one of the biggest A.C. shopping complexes with residential apartments.

CHAPTER SIX

RECOGNITIONS GALORE

Mr Rajesh Singh has constantly worked hard towards a sustainable society by creating new opportunities, employment for youth, and constant community welfare. According to him, "Human life attains its true fulfilment when the struggle of existence gets transformed into a meaningful pursuit, and education is undeniably the most potent tool to bring about this information. Each individual is born with some inherent talent, and it is through education this talent gets nurtured, encouraged, and sharpened to find its most creative expression.

The test of education, therefore, lies in how effectively it unshackles the human mind, ignites curiosity, promotes the spirit of inquiry and unleashes the creative impulse of a student to help him realise their full potential."

A renowned social activist, his commitment to culture has helped thousands of poor and backward families live better lives.

A true visionary with a vision to provide free access to Education for all, Mr Rajesh Singh provides Free Education to 25 per cent of the total strength at Kunwar's Global School to students belonging to backward and underprivileged strata of society. Beginning with a small house colony project in Varanasi in the late 90s and now, after six years, the group is considered a promoter of the best housing colony and commercial premises in both the cities.

His recognitions include the following via pictures:

The life.... different faces... different phases: Blessings on the way!

Powered by
TATA MOTORS
Connecting Aspirations

GOLD ICON

DAINIK JAGRAN-INEXT
proudly recognizes

MR. RAJESH SINGH
Chairman, Kunwar's Global School

as the Gold Icon, honours the inspiring success story and his magnificent role towards spreading light in the education sector. We laud him for his contribution towards upliftment of society and nation building at large.

We sincerely appreciate him for illuminating the path of learning with his vision and creating a paradigm shift in education, together with progress of the region and its people.

It is an absolute pleasure for us to engage with such an icon in the field of Education, in the real sense.

Alok Sanwal
Chief Operating Officer
Dainik Jagran-inext

2. Awarded at ZEE UP/UK Conclave by Hon'ble CM UP Shri Yogi Adityanath Ji to impart social and educational service in the district

3. Lucknow University Alumni Foundation as distinguished Alumni Award by Shri Ram Naik, Honble Governor of Uttar Pradesh

Dainik
Bhaskar.com
World's No.1 Hindi News Website
PRESENTS
VISIONARIES
OF UTTAR PRADESH
EDITION : 2017
Award For
CONTRIBUTING IN THE INCLUSIVE GROWTH &
PLAYING A SIGNIFICANT ROLE IN SOCIO-ECONOMIC WELLBEING OF
THE STATE OF UTTAR PRADESH
TO
SHRI. RAJESH SING
(CHAIRMAN)
KUNWAR'S GLOBAL SCHOOL (DAYAL GROUP)
AS THE VISIONARY OF UTTAR PRADESH
OUR ESTEEMED CHIEF GUEST FOR THE CEREMONY
DR. DINESH SHARMA JI
Hon'ble Deputy Chief Minister
Government of Uttar Pradesh
SHRI. KESHAV PRASAD MAURYA JI
Hon'ble Deputy Chief Minister
Government of Uttar Pradesh

LETTER OF COMMENDATION

Dainik Jagran inext

Radio City

UP RATAN SAMMAN 2019

is given to

MR. RAJESH SINGH

Kunwar's Global School

for his magnificent contribution towards the upliftment of the state, society and nation building at large

by

YOGI ADITYA NATH

Hon'ble Chief Minister, Uttar Pradesh

SHAILESH GUPTA

6. Bharat Samachar Excellence of Education Award 2019 for outstanding and exemplary contribution towards Education by Shri Dinesh Sharma ji Deputy Chief Minister of Uttar Pradesh

MMA
2021
BHN News
कुंवर्स ग्लोबल स्कूल के चेयरमैन राजेश सिंह को यूपी रत्न से नावाज़ा गया, केंद्रीय मंत्री स्मृति ईरानी ने दिया अवार्ड - BHN News
Visit

Awarded Honorary Doctorate in the field of Social Service

Mahatma Gandhi Samman by NRI Welfare Society of India in recognition of contribution and dedication to worthy causes and achievements in keeping the flag of India High at house of Common, London

राजेश सिंह यूपी रत्न अवार्ड से सम्मानित

लखनऊ। उप्र की राजधानी लखनऊ के एकमात्र बोर्डिंग स्कूल कुंवर्स ग्लोबल स्कूल के चेयरमैन राजेश सिंह को यूपी रत्न अवार्ड से सम्मानित किया गया है। यह अवार्ड उन्हें देश व समाज के उत्थान में उनके शानदार योगदान के लिए उप्र के सबसे प्रगतिशील विद्यालय की श्रेणी में दिया गया। राजेश सिंह को यह अवार्ड केंद्रीय महिला व बाल विकास मंत्री स्मृति ईरानी के कर कमलों द्वारा प्रदान किया गया। यह यूपी रत्न अवार्ड एक समूह की तरफ से दिया गया है। अवार्ड प्राप्त होने से अभिभूत राजेश सिंह ने कहा कि कुंवर्स ग्लोबल स्कूल को हमने एक ऐसे विद्यालय के रूप में विकसित किया है जिसमें बच्चे के सम्पूर्ण व्यक्तित्व के विकास का प्रयास रहता है। राजेश सिंह ने कहा हमारा मानना है कि हर बच्चे में कोई न कोई ऐसी विशेषता होती है जिसे आगे लाना हमारा कर्तव्य है।

NEXT TOPLINE

DAINIK JAGRAN I NEXT CONNECT MARKETING INITIATIVE

समाज को देना ही सबकुछ होता है राजेश सिंह

बच्चे के सर्वांगीण विकास में खेल का अहम रोल

भास्कर ब्यूरो

कोरोना ने बच्चों के सर्वांगीण विकास पर काफी नकारात्मक असर डाला है। यहां हमें समझने की जरूरत है कि खेल बच्चों को मानसिक और शारीरिक दोनों तरह से अच्छा सोचने में मदद करता है। इसलिए, बचपन से ही अपने दैनिक रूटीन में खेल को शामिल करना बेहद जरूरी है। प्रसिद्ध शिक्षाविद और कुंवर्स ग्लोबल स्कूल के संस्थापक एवं प्रबंध निदेशक राजेश कुमार सिंह कहते हैं कि खेलों में हिस्सा लेने से बच्चों में शारीरिक कौशल का विकास होता है, नियमित तौर पर व्यायाम होता है, टीम सदस्य बनने की सीख मिलती है, निष्पक्षता के साथ खेलने की सीख हासिल होती है, आत्मसम्मान में सुधार आता है और साथ ही आनंद मिलता है।

खेल हमेशा से इंसान को स्वस्थ, तरोताजा, एकजुट और प्रसन्न रहने में मददगार रहे हैं और बच्चों, युवाओं, वयस्कों और बुजुर्गों को कई तरह के फायदे प्रदान करते हैं। कुंवर्स ग्लोबल स्कूल के संस्थापक एवं प्रबंध निदेशक राजेश कुमार सिंह बच्चों के शारीरिक और मानसिक विकास में खेलों का योगदान को इस प्रकार चिह्नित करते हैं-

किशोरों की तरह बच्चे भी तनाव के उच्च स्तर से गुजरते हैं। यदि यह तनाव बचपन में ही दूर न किया जाए तो इससे गंभीर अवसाद की समस्या पैदा हो सकती है। नियमित व्यायाम, फील-गुड केमिकल रिलीज करने से दिमाग के कुछ हिस्सों को सक्रिय बनाया जा सकता है जिससे चिंता और अवसाद दूर करने में मदद मिलती है। इसलिए जब बच्चा सक्रियता के साथ खेलता है तो वे प्रभावी तरीके से अवसाद के स्तर को दूर करने में सक्षम होता है।

What great personalities speak about him?

Amitabh Bacchan - Actor
I am overwhelmed by the act of charity and sacrifice by Mr. Rajesh Singh. I thank him to bring such positive & major change in the society

With the "the Flying Sikh" Late Milkha Singh

Anupam Kher- Actor
I have hardly seen such infrastructure in recent decade Such charity and social service needs shear passion for the society

Governor of UP - Shri Ram Naik
I Congratulate Mr, Rajesh Singh for keeping such philanthropical ideas and initiating such charitable education school

Dr. Mahendra Singh - I am proud of the social services Rajesh Singh is involved in. His initiatives are helpful for the government also. I wish him all the luck and blessings

Chief Minister of UP - Yogi Adityanath Ji
Appreciation for selfless service during Kumbh 2019

Social Activist - Anna Hazare
Bina kisi lobh ke samaj k liye kiya jane wala karya sarahniya hai - Rajesh singh ko badhai

CHAPTER SEVEN

IN PRESS- MEDIA

References/ Resource:

Kunwar's Global School - intelligence beyond boundaries
Read more At:
https://www.aninews.in/news/business/business/kunwars-global-school-intelligence-beyond-boundaries201901081623110001/

Rajesh Singh, Chairman - Kunwar's Global School

Kunwar's Global School - intelligence beyond boundaries

ANI | Updated: Jan 08, 2019 16:27 IST

A philanthropist and society up-lifter – Mr. Rajesh Kumar Singh

Mr. Rajesh Singh converted his 100 crore land initially allocated for a 5-star club into an educational institute, that aims to provide education to children belonging to rural areas, and more specifically, to underprivileged classes of the society.

Five reasons why sport is important in early childhood

Rajesh Kumar Singh
Founder and MD
Kunwar's Global School

Sport breaks every barrier. The benefits are many from making one feel good about themselves, improves self-esteem, and most importantly, those who involve in sport have fun. The enhancement of children's mental and physical growth and development is undoubtedly the most important contribution of sports. However, the list of values children may acquire and learn from sports is way too long. There are many other positive aspects of playing sports, which reveals its true beauty.

Inducting young children into sport at an early age has numerous benefits for their overall growth and development. Sport has brought health, freshness, unity and happiness to human beings for years, offering a number of benefits to children, young, adults and old. However, the contribution of sports towards the physical and mental growth and development of children can be reviewed as its greatest outcome.

Five reasons why sports is important in early childhood

1. Promotes good health

Many studies state that from a young age living an active lifestyle and following a healthy routine can lower the chances of getting serious medical issues like obesity, diabetes, weak bones and issues with cholesterol and blood pressure later in life.

CHAPTER EIGHT

The Quality Mantras

The Quality mantras reflect learning as a priority. Rajesh Singh's attributes towards the successful venture make every challenge an opportunity and convert it to a successful story. Here are some of his quality mantras that activate priority-based reflections of life as a lesson in itself.

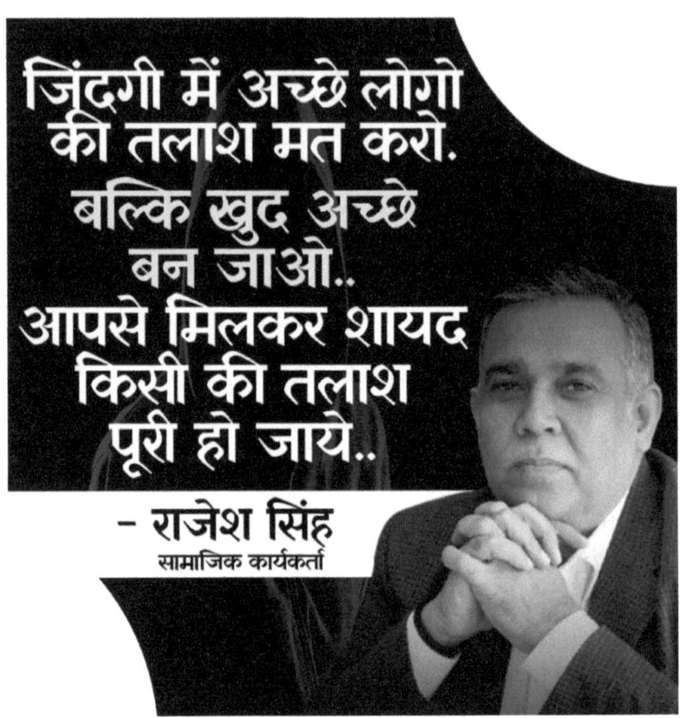
जिंदगी में अच्छे लोगो
की तलाश मत करो.
बल्कि खुद अच्छे
बन जाओ..
आपसे मिलकर शायद
किसी की तलाश
पूरी हो जाये..
- राजेश सिंह
सामाजिक कार्यकर्ता

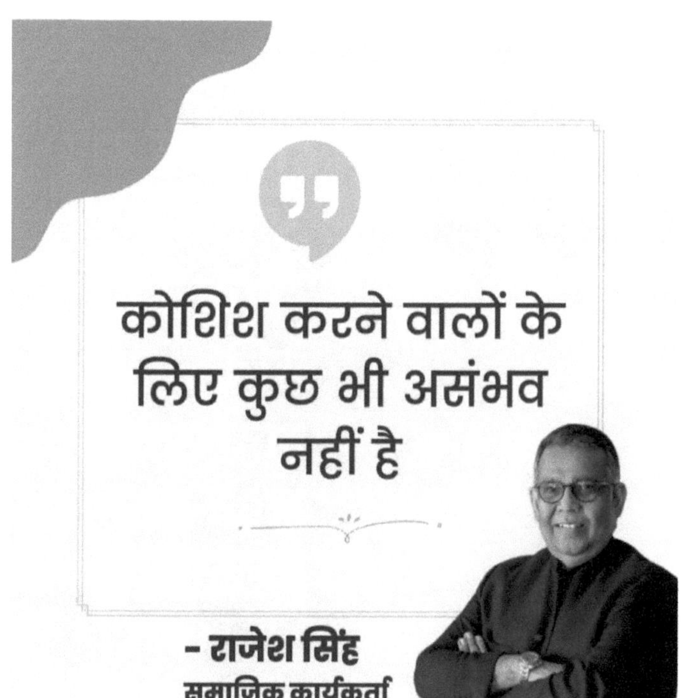
कोशिश करने वालों के लिए कुछ भी असंभव नहीं है
- राजेश सिंह
समाजिक कार्यकर्ता

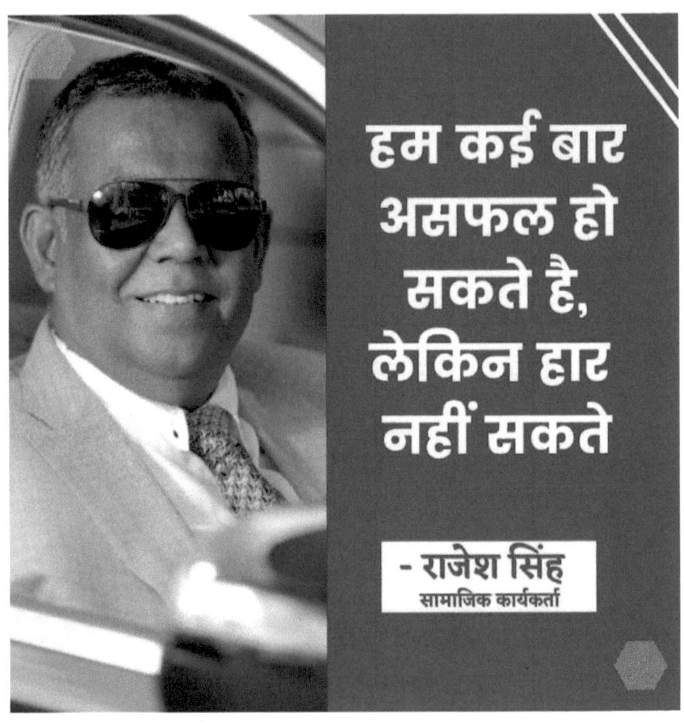
हम कई बार
असफल हो
सकते है,
लेकिन हार
नहीं सकते
- राजेश सिंह
सामाजिक कार्यकर्ता

किसी को दुखी न करना ही खुश रहने को एकमात्र उपाय है
राजेश सिंह
सामाजिक कार्यकर्ता

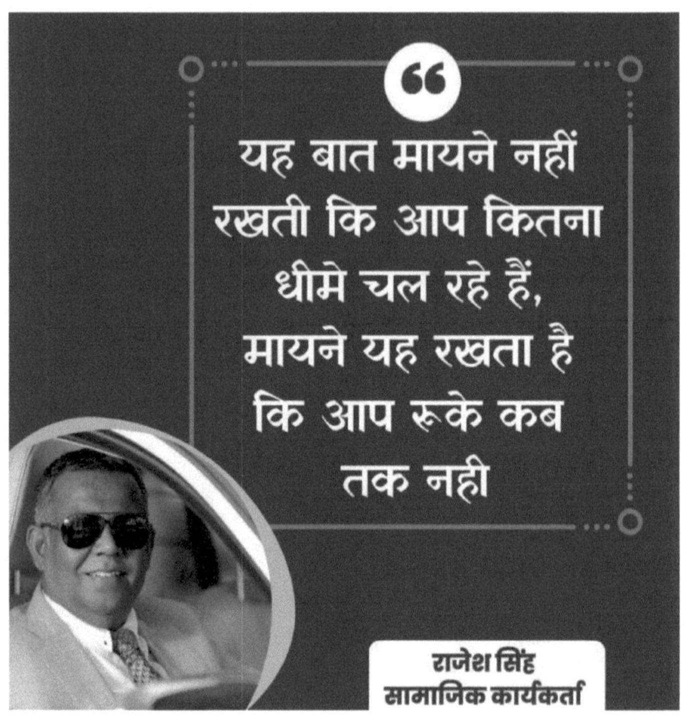
यह बात मायने नहीं
रखती कि आप कितना
धीमे चल रहे हैं,
मायने यह रखता है
कि आप रूके कब
तक नही
राजेश सिंह
सामाजिक कार्यकर्ता

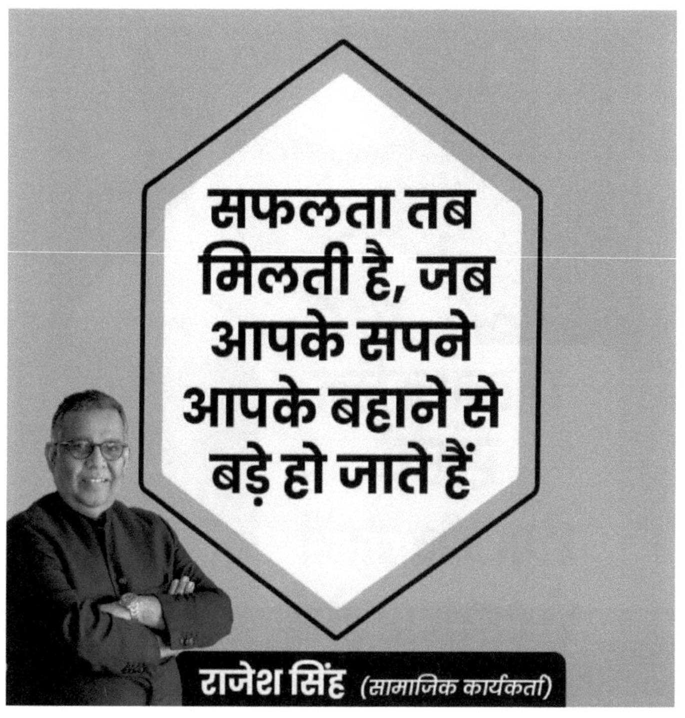
सफलता तब
मिलती है, जब
आपके सपने
आपके बहाने से
बड़े हो जाते हैं
राजेश सिंह (सामाजिक कार्यकर्ता)

जितना कठिन
संघर्ष
होगा जीत उतनी
ही शानदार होगी
राजेश सिंह
सामाजिक कार्यकर्ता

इससे पहले की सपने सच हों आपको सपने देखने होंगे
राजेश सिंह
सामाजिक कार्यकर्ता

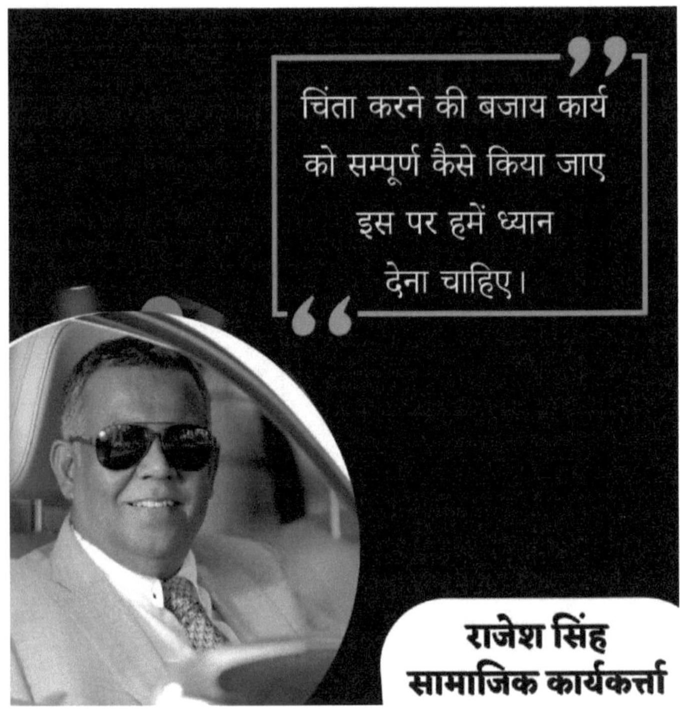
चिंता करने की बजाय कार्य
को सम्पूर्ण कैसे किया जाए
इस पर हमें ध्यान
देना चाहिए।
राजेश सिंह
सामाजिक कार्यकर्त्ता

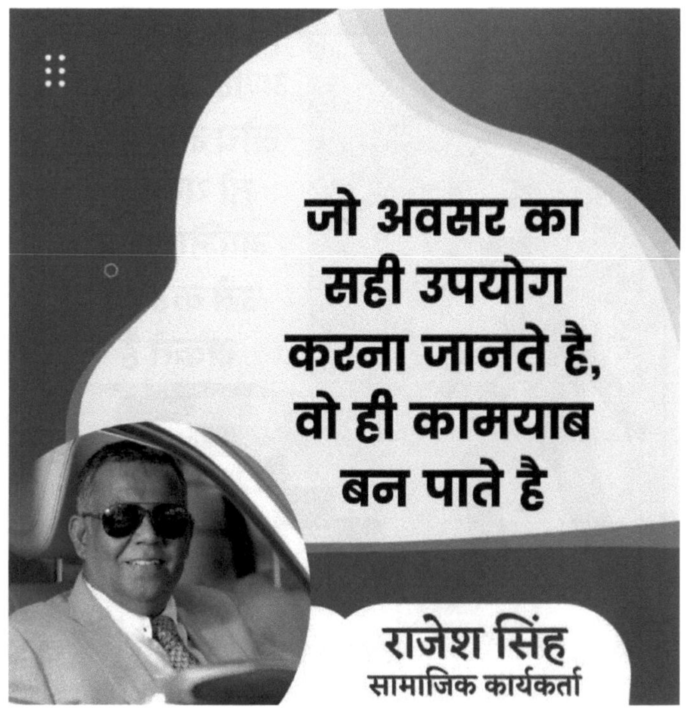
जो अवसर का
सही उपयोग
करना जानते है,
वो ही कामयाब
बन पाते है
राजेश सिंह
सामाजिक कार्यकर्ता

अगर आप कुछ सोच सकते हैं, तो यकीन मानिए आप उसे कर भी सकते हैं
राजेश सिंह (सामाजिक कार्यकर्ता)

Source: Social Media

CHAPTER NINE

THE MISSION & VISION OF KGS

The chairman, Rajesh Singh, believes that learning is a priority. The campus showcases quality learning with an emphasis on Experiential Learning. As per him, Kunwar's Global School, Lucknow, is the first international school of its kind in Lucknow. The school activates an essential role in preparing community leaders in science, arts, business, industry, politics and sports.

He believes that:

"At Kunwar's Global School, we aim at making children capable of becoming responsible and productive members of a global society. Here, children's knowledge, skills, and attitudes are taught through learning experiences and opportunities created for them in the school. In the classroom, learners can analyse and evaluate their experiences, learn to doubt, question, investigate, and be driven to think independently."

www.kunwarsglobalschool.com

The school's mission is:

- *To achieve excellence in academics.*
- *To uphold integrity, charity, courtesy, and respect for self and others generate qualities of acceptance, peaceful co-existence and tolerance, abide by the nation's constitution and respect its ideal and institutions.*
- *To promote harmony.*

“In the beginning, God created the earth, and he looked upon it in His cosmic loneliness.

And God said, "Let Us make living creatures out of mud, so the mud can see what We have done." And God created every living creature that now moveth, and one was a man. Mud as man alone could speak. God leaned close to mud as man sat up, looked around, and spoke. Man blinked. "What is the purpose of all this?" he asked politely.

"Everything must have a purpose?" asked God.

"Certainly," said the man.

"Then I leave it to you to think of one for all this," said God.

And He went away."
— Kurt Vonnegut, Cat's Cradle

About The Author

Dheeraj Mehrotra has been honoured with the President of India's National Teacher Award in the year 2006 and the Best Science Teacher State Award, Innovation in Education for his inception of Six Sigma In Education by Education Watch, New Delhi and Education World- Best Teacher Award, BOLT Learner Teacher Award by Air India, 'Innovation in Education Award 2016' among others. He has developed over 150 FREE EDUCATIONAL MOBILE Apps for the Google Play Store exclusively for Teachers, Students, and Parents. This work has been recognized by the LIMCA BOOK OF RECORDS & INDIA BOOK OF RECORDS as the only Indian to draw that feast. Dr Mehrotra is presently working as a PRINCIPAL at KUNWARS GLOBAL SCHOOL, Lucknow, in India. He is

an active TEDx speaker. As a premium UDEMY Instructor, he has also developed over 450 courses and is catering to over 8 Lakh students from 180 plus countries. He can be visited at www.authordheerajmehrotra.com

Printed by Libri Plureos GmbH in Hamburg, Germany